# JOHN DENVER
# AUTOGRAPH

| | |
|---|---|
| 53 | AMERICAN CHILD |
| 60 | AUTOGRAPH |
| 22 | THE BALLAD OF ST. ANNE'S REEL |
| 4 | DANCING WITH THE MOUNTAINS |
| 8 | HOW MOUNTAIN GIRLS CAN LOVE |
| 45 | IN MY HEART |
| 17 | THE MOUNTAIN SONG |
| 14 | SONG FOR THE LIFE |
| 48 | YOU SAY THAT THE BATTLE IS OVER |
| 40 | WHALEBONES AND CROSSES |
| 28 | WRANGELL MOUNTAIN SONG |
| 3 | PERFORMANCE NOTES |
| 34 | LYRICS |

*Edited by Milton Okun*

Associate Music Editor - Dan Fox

© Copyright 1980 Cherry Lane Music Co., Inc.
International Copyright Secured   All Rights Reserved

ISBN 0-89524-085-8

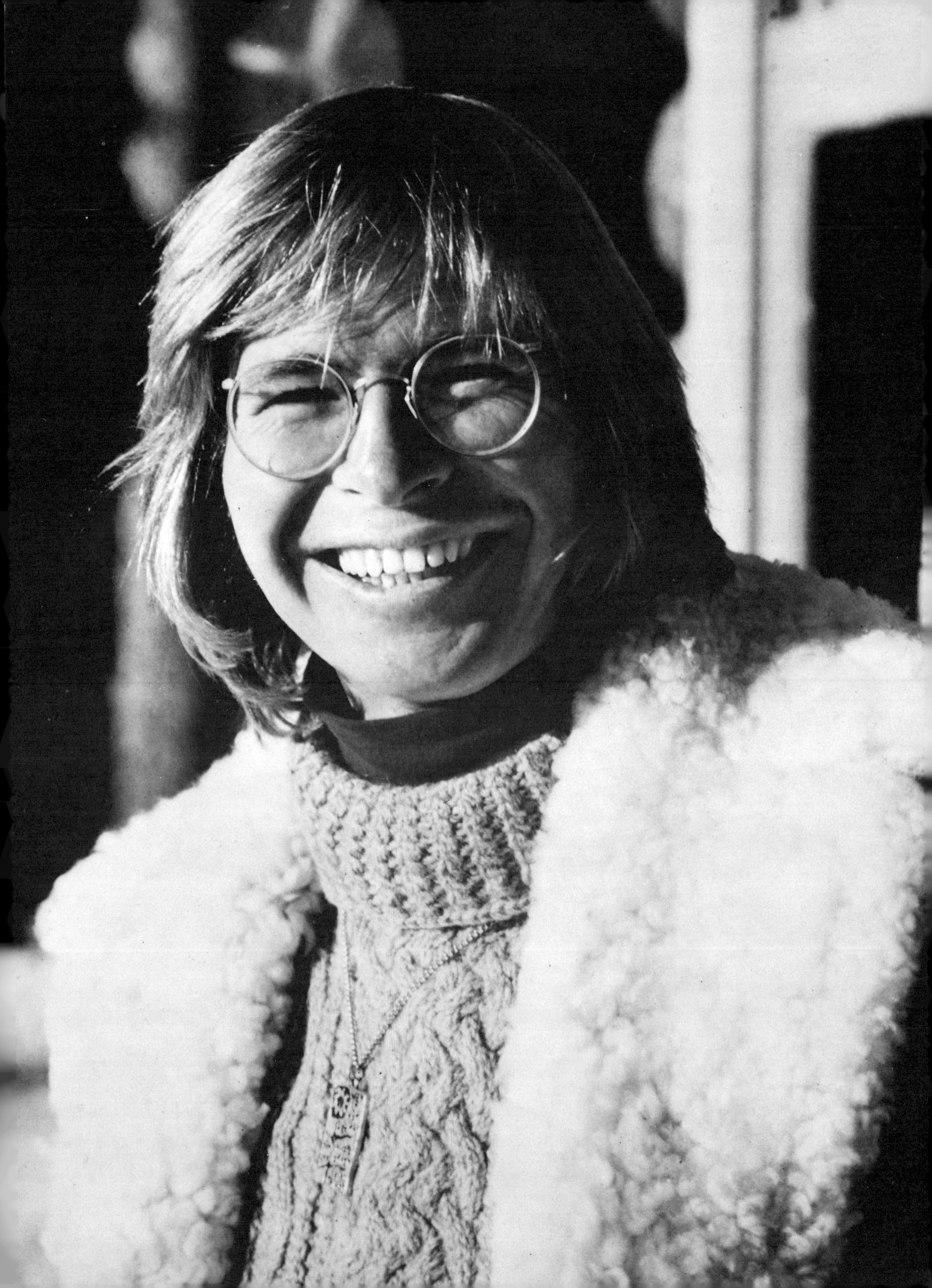

## PERFORMANCE NOTES

John Denver's songbooks are always full of good, singable and playable songs. This folio, matching John's latest album *Autograph*, is no exception. As is this publisher's policy, all the arrangements are bar-for-bar transcriptions, allowing you to play along with the record if desired.

Pianists should be aware that the small grace notes often found in the right hand represent either alternative vocal lines (where a second verse differs from the first) or vocal embellishments, and are to be sung, not played. In this way we can accurately indicate John's vocal style without making the piano part unnecessarily complicated.

Since John's music is rooted firmly in the country and western and folk traditions, the written arrangements should not be interpreted too strictly. For example, 8th notes are generally played with a swing feeling (more or less like ♩³♪), rather than the strict interpretation given by classical musicians. Judicious use of the pedal is indicated to simulate the feeling of a live performance enhanced with electronic instruments.

Guitarists will note that we have taken special care with the chord diagrams. Each diagram in this book has been stamped in individually, allowing us to notate precisely such nice touches as the descending bass lines on *Autograph*, *Wrangell Mountain Song*, and *Song For The Life*, as well as the interesting chord sequence on *The Mountain Song*, and the impressionistic harmonies of *Whalebones And Crosses*.

Also of interest is the D tuning used on *Dancing With The Mountains*. The 6th string is lowered a full tone to D, enabling the player to get unusually full sounding chords in this key. In two cases capo instructions direct the guitarist to play in a different key than the pianist. *Wrangell Mountain Song* is recorded in A; by placing the capo up two frets from the G formation, the guitar still sounds in A, but the chord formations in G fit the hand better. (See example below from *Wrangell Mountain Song*, p. 28*).

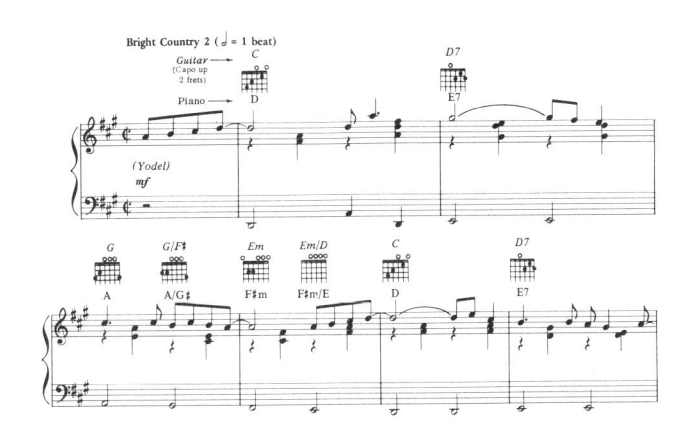

The capo in *You Say That The Battle Is Over* serves a different purpose. By moving the capo up five frets to the key of C from the G formation, the guitar is placed in a high-pitched range reminiscent of the Latin American "quatro," a small guitar often used in mariachi bands.

Although all the songs can be played either pick or finger style, we suggest the pick for *American Child*, *The Ballad Of St. Anne's Reel*, *How Mountain Girls Can Love*, *The Mountain Song*, *You Say That The Battle Is Over*, and *Dancing With The Mountains*. The other songs sound better when played finger style.

\* © Copyright 1976 Cherry Lane Music Co.
This arrangement © Copyright 1980 Cherry Lane Music Co.
International Copyright Secured    All Rights Reserved

# DANCING WITH THE MOUNTAINS

Words and Music by
John Denver

Medium Disco Beat

*Guitarists: Tune 6th string to D

© Copyright 1979 Cherry Lane Music Co.
This arrangement © Copyright 1980 Cherry Lane Music Co.
International Copyright Secured    All Rights Reserved

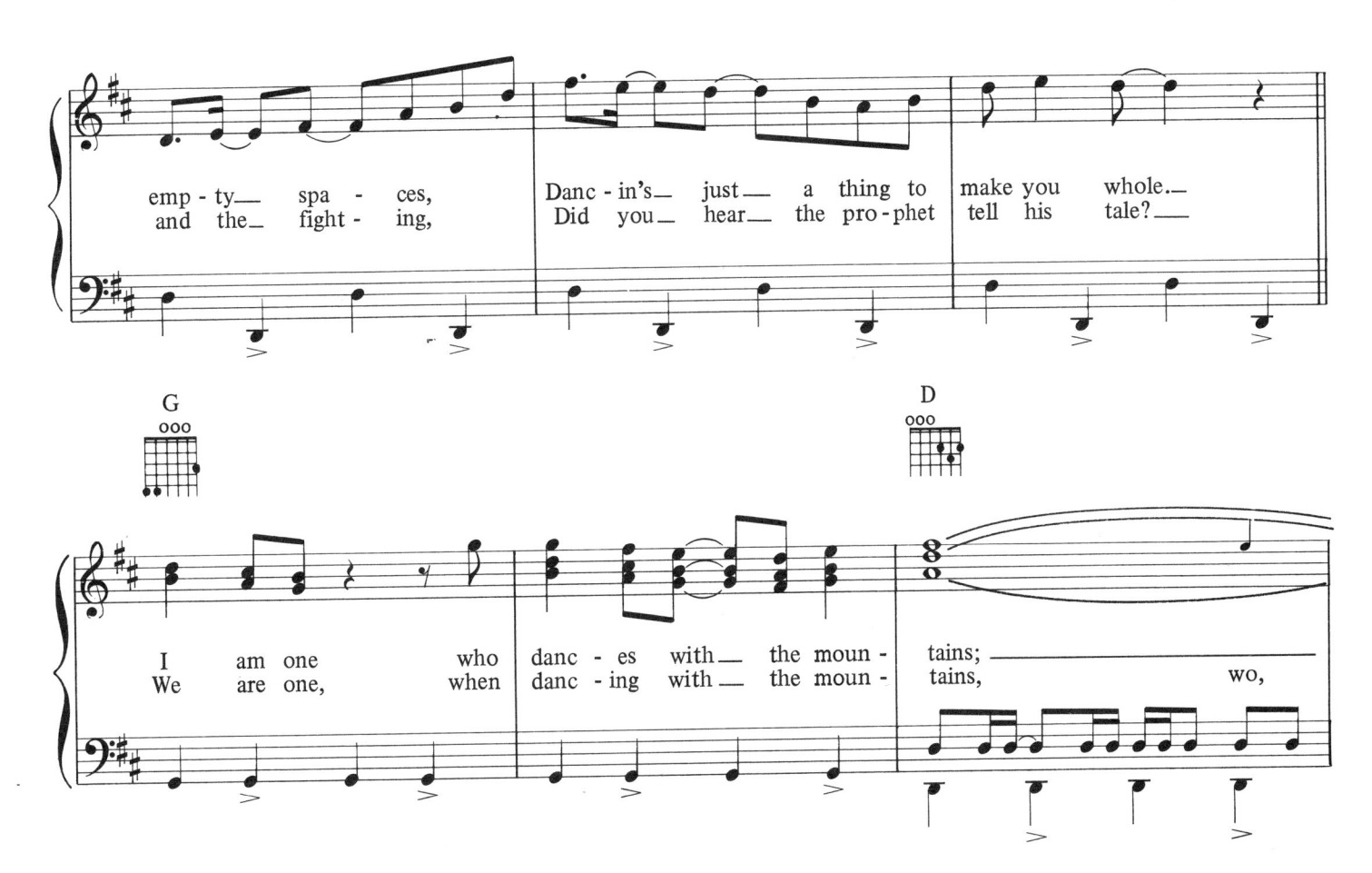

stretch your soul. Just re - lax\_\_ and let the rhy - thm\_\_ take\_\_ you,
Were you\_\_ there\_\_ the night they lost the\_\_ light - ning?

Don't you\_\_ be\_\_ a - fraid to lose con - trol.\_\_ If your\_\_ heart\_\_ has found some
Were you\_\_ there\_\_ the day the earth stood still?\_\_ Did you\_\_ see\_\_ the fa - mous

emp - ty\_\_ spa - ces, Danc - in's\_\_ just\_\_ a thing to make you whole.\_\_
and the\_\_ fight - ing, Did you\_\_ hear\_\_ the pro - phet tell his tale?\_\_

G     D

I am one, who danc - es with\_\_ the moun - tains;
We are one, when danc - ing with\_\_ the moun - tains, wo,

wo;

I am one — who danc-es in — the wind, —
We are one, — who sing-ing in — the wind, —

wo, wo, wo;

I am one — who
We are one, — when

danc - es on — the o - cean, wo, wo, My
think-ing of — each oth - er More than

part - ner's — more than piec - es, more than friends.

*Final fade omitted

# HOW MOUNTAIN GIRLS CAN LOVE

Fast country beat (in 2)

Words and Music by
Ruby Rakes

1. Get at 'em boys, _____ Go back home,
2. (Inst.)

back to the girl you love.

© Copyright 1958 Fort Knox Music Company
This arrangement © Copyright 1980 Fort Knox Music Company
International Copyright Secured   Used by Permission   All Rights Reserved

D
A
Treat her right, never wrong,
E
A
How moun - tain girls can love.
There's a
(Verses)
A
1. Rid - in at night in a high cold wind on the
2. lake in the hills where my true love goes,
E
A
trail of the old lone - some pine,
That's when she's think - in' of me.

Thinkin' of you baby, feelin' so blue, wond'rin' why I left you behind.
Why I'm not there only heaven knows, Heaven knows that's where I'd rather be.

*Chorus*
Get at 'em boys, Go back home,

back to the girl you love. Treat her right, never wrong, How mountain girls can love.

*Instrumentals*

Get at 'em boys —— Go back home, Back to the girl you love.

Treat her right, —— never wrong, How moun- tain girls can love.

# SONG FOR THE LIFE

Words and Music by
Rodney Crowell

Funky three

I don't drink as much as I used to,
But don't they Late-ly it just ain't my style,
And the hard times don't hurt like they ought to,
They pass quick-er like when I's a child.

Mid-sum-mer days sit so heav-y,
flow like a breeze thru your mind,
And nothin' oc-curs in a hur-ry
To make up for some-one's lost time.

Chorus:

Some - how___ I've learned how to lis - ten___ (last time) For a sound like the { sun go - in' down. / breeze dy - in' down. } In the mag - ic the morn - ing___ is bring - ing There's a song { for the life I have found.___ / for a friend I have found.___ / for the life I have found.___ }

G7/D
C
D7
It keeps my feet on the
She keeps my feet on the
She keeps my feet on the
1.2.
G
D7
3.
G
ground.
ground.
2. Don't the
3. (Inst.)
ground,
D/F♯
Em
G7/D
C
D7
G
That keeps my feet on the ground.
Slower

# THE MOUNTAIN SONG

Words and Music by
Tracey Wickland

Slowly

*mf*

I came here from the city___ A thousand miles___ away___ I came just for a little while You know I never meant___ to stay___ I meant to take___ my pleasure Have a good time___ and be gone But I

© Copyright 1977 Cherry Lane Music Co.
This arrangement © Copyright 1980 Cherry Lane Music Co.
International Copyright Secured    All Rights Reserved

| Dm | A/E | Bm7 E | A |

fell in love with a lady. Now I sing a moun-tain song. I

| A | Amaj7 | A7 | D |

lis-tened to the mu-sic Of the night wind in the pines I

| Dm | A/E | Bm7 | E |

saw the qui-et splen-dor Of a field of col-um-bine I

| A | Amaj7 | A7 | D |

skied on crys-tal path-ways To a moun-tain peak so tall And I walked the might-y sum-mits with the one who made it all_____ And I

fell in love__ with a la-dy 'cause I've seen her__ at her best__ And I've walked__
fall in love__ with a la-dy when you've slept up-on her breast__ When you've

___ her wild__ and rug-ged paths__ thru her o-pen wil-der-ness__ And now I
walked her wild__ and rug-ged paths__ To her o-pen wil-der-ness__ And you

nev-er can be-tray__ her, steal her rich-es___ and be gone__ } 'cause when you
nev-er can be-tray__ her, steal her rich-es___ and be gone__    'cause when you

love a moun - tain la - dy you're gon - na sing a moun - tain song
love a moun - tain la - dy you got - ta sing a moun - tain song

*Instrumental (relaxed)*

3. Now

peo - ple come from ev - 'ry - where\_\_ To see what they\_\_ can find\_\_ And

some take lots of pic - tures And some just take their time But there's

some who take\_\_ her beau - ty That can't be bought or sold\_\_ And they

think of on - ly mon - ey While des - troy-ing wealth un-told\_\_ But you

*D.S. and fade on instrumental*

# THE BALLAD OF ST. ANNE'S REEL

Adaptation and additional music
and lyric by David Mallett

cof - fee and a tin - y trace of fid - dlin' in the dis-tance far be - hind him.

dime a - cross the coun - ter then, A shy hel - lo, a brand new friend, And a walk a - long the street in the win - try
now his feet be - gin to tap, A little boy says, "I'll take your hat." He's caught up, in the mag - ic of her
sail - or's gone, the room is bare, The old pi - a - no's set - tin' there And some - one's hat's left hang - in' on the

weath - er. _____   A yel - low light, __ an
smile. _____   And leap, the heart __ in the
rack. _____   And emp - ty chairs, __ in the

o - pen door, __ And a "Wel - come, friend, __ there's room for more." __ And
side him went, __ And off a - cross the floor he sent __ His
wood - en floor __ That feels the touch __ of shoes no more, __ A -

then they're stand - in' there in - side to - geth - er. _____
clum - sy bod - y, grace - ful as a child. _____
wait - in' for the danc - ers to come back. _____

He said, "I've heard that tune be - fore __ some - where, But I
He said, "There's mag - ic in the fid - dler's arm, And there's
And the fid - dle's in the clos - et of some __

| can't re - mem - ber when.___ | Was it on some oth - er |
| mag - ic in___ this town;___ There's | mag - ic in the |
| daugh - ter of___ the town;___ The | strings are broke, and the |

| friend - ly shore___ or did I | hear it on the wind?___ | Was it |
| danc - er's feet,___ And the | way they put them down." | |
| bow is gone,___ And the | cov - er's but - toned down.___ | But___ |

| writ - ten on___ the | sky a - bove?___ I think I | heard it from___ some - |
| Peo - ple smil - ing | ev - 'ry - where,___ | boots and rib - bons, |
| some - times on___ De - | cem - ber nights___ when the | air is cold___ and the |

| one I loved.___ But I | nev - er heard___ it sound___ | so sweet |
| locks of hair,___ | laugh - ter and old blue suits___ | and Eas - ter |
| wind is right,___ There's a | mel - o - dy___ that pass - es | through this |

gowns. since then." (Fiddle)
town.

2. And

3. Now the

*D.S. al Coda*

27

# WRANGELL MOUNTAIN SONG

Words and Music by
John Denver

(Yodel)

Sunday, and it's rain-in' in A-las-ka, Sev-en days I hav-en't seen the sun.

© Copyright 1976 Cherry Lane Music Co.
This arrangement © Copyright 1980 Cherry Lane Music Co.
International Copyright Secured    All Rights Reserved

Fly-in' bush, fly-in' low a-long the shore-line, Do-in' ev-'ry-thing I can to make it home. I can't wait to see the Wran-gell Moun-tains.

C D7
D E7
I can't wait to do what I will do.
G C
A D
Hon-ey, did I nev-
D7 G G/F♯ Em Em/D
E7 A A/G♯ F♯m F♯m/E
-er say how time goes by so slow-ly When I
C C/B Am D7 G
D D/C♯ Bm E7 A
can't wait to get back home to you.

Three years from the war and settled down now, I did my time and served my country well. In the freedom I defended I don't know a better way to feel. I can't wait

Carthy lies asleep beside the glacier, It's colder now, winter's in the air. If you think they're wild It's just because they can't be broken, It's a strong and gentle people livin' there.

C D G
D E A
to see the Wran - gell Moun - tains. I can't wait
C D7 G
D E7 A
to do what I will do.
C D7 G G/F♯ Em Em/D
D E7 A A/G♯ F♯m F♯m/E
Hon - ey, did I nev - er say how time goes by so slow - ly When I
C C/B Am D7 To Coda G
D D/C♯ Bm E7 A
can't wait to get back home to you. It's a qui -

Em
C
G
F♯m
D
A
- et life_ out here a - mong the moun - tains_ In a cab -
Em
A7
D7
F♯m
B7
E7
D.S. al Coda
- in that was built_ with these two hands._ Mc
Coda
G
C
D7
G
G/F♯
A
D
E7
A
A/G♯
you._ (Yodel)
Em
Em/D
C
C/B
Am
D7
G
D7
G
F♯m
F♯m/E
D
D/C♯
Bm
E7
A
E7
A

**DANCING WITH THE MOUNTAINS**
(John Denver)

*Everybody's got the dancin' fever*
*Everybody loves to rock and roll*
*Play it louder baby play it faster*
*Funky music gotta stretch your soul*

*Just relax and let the rhythm take you*
*Don't you be afraid to lose control*
*If your heart has found some empty spaces*
*Dancin's just a thing to make you whole*

   *I am one who dances with the mountains*
   *I am one who dances in the wind*
   *I am one who dances on the ocean*
   *My partners more than pieces more than friends*

*Were you there the night they lost the lightning*
*Were you there the day the earth stood still*
*Did you see the famous and the fighting*
*Did you hear the prophet tell his tale*

   *We are one when dancing with the mountains*
   *We are one when singing in the wind*
   *We are one when thinking of each other*
   *More than partners much more than pieces more*
     *than friends*

© 1979 Cherry Lane Music Co. (ASCAP)
Used by permission. All rights reserved.

---

   'The Mountain Song' is dedicated to all those who realize that we must draw the line somewhere—that sometimes what is on the surface of our beautiful Mother Earth is much more valuable than that which lies beneath it. This song is especially for our friends in Crested Butte, Colorado.
Thank you, Tracey.

*John*

**THE MOUNTAIN SONG**
(Tracey Wickland)

*I came here from the city*
*A thousand miles away*
*I came just for a little while*
*You know I never meant to stay*
*I meant to take my pleasure*
*Have a good time and be gone*
*But I fell in love with a lady*
*Now I sing a mountain song*

*I listened to the music*
*Of the night wind in the pines*
*I saw the quiet splendor*
*Of a field of columbine*
*I skied on crystal pathways*
*To a mountain peak so tall*
*And I walked the mighty summits*
*With the one who made it all*

   *And I fell in love with a lady*
   *'Cause I've seen her at her best*
   *And I've walked her wild and rugged paths*
   *Through her open wilderness*
   *And now I never can betray her*
   *Steal her riches and be gone*
   *'Cause when you love a mountain lady*
   *You're gonna sing a mountain song*

*Now people come from everywhere*
*To see what they can find*
*And some take lots of pictures*
*And some just take their time*
*But they're some who take her beauty*
*That can't be bought or sold*
*And they think of only money*
*While destroying wealth untold*

   *But you fall in love with a lady*
   *When you've slept upon her breast*
   *When you've walked her wild and rugged paths*
   *To her open wilderness*
   *And you never can betray her*
   *Steal her riches and be gone*
   *'Cause when you love a mountain lady*
   *You gotta sing a mountain song*

© 1977 Cherry Lane Music Co. (ASCAP)
Used by permission. All rights reserved.

**HOW MOUNTAIN GIRLS CAN LOVE**
(Ruby Rakes)

    Get at 'em boys, go back home
    Back to the girl you love
    Treat her right, never wrong
    How mountain girls can love

Ridin' at night in a high cold wind
On the trail of the old lonesome pine
Thinking of you baby
Feelin' so blue
Wondering why I left you behind

    Get at 'em boys, go back home
    Back to the girl you love
    Treat her right, never wrong
    How mountain girls can love

There's a lake in the hills
Where my true love goes
That's when she's thinkin' of me
Why I'm not there only heaven knows
Heaven knows that's where I'd rather be

    Get at 'em boys, go back home
    Back to the girl you love
    Treat her right, never wrong
    How mountain girls can love

© 1958 Fort Knox Music Company (BMI)

**WRANGELL MOUNTAIN SONG**
(John Denver)

Sunday and it's rainin' in Alaska
Seven days I haven't seen the sun
Flyin' bush, flyin' low along the shoreline
Doin' everything I can to make it home

    I can't wait to see the Wrangell Mountains
    I can't wait to do what I will do
    Honey, did I never say
    How time goes by so slowly
    When I can't wait to get back home to you

Three years from the war and settled down now
I did my time and served my country well
In the freedom I defended
I fly beneath the North Star
And I just don't know a better way to feel

    I can't wait to see the Wrangell Mountains
    I can't wait to do what I will do
    Honey, did I never say
    How time goes by so slowly
    When I can't wait to get back home to you

      It's a quiet life out here among the mountains
      In a cabin that was built with these two hands

McCarthy lies asleep beside the glacier
It's colder now, winter's in the air
If you think they're wild
It's just because they can't be broken
It's a strong and gentle people livin' there

    I can't wait to see the Wrangell Mountains
    I can't wait to do what I will do
    Honey, did I never say
    How time goes by so slowly
    When I can't wait to get back home to you

© 1976 Cherry Lane Music Co. (ASCAP)
Used by permission. All rights reserved.

The Alaska songs are dedicated to all the people in Alaska... the Eskimos, Aleuts and all the men and women who emigrated from the Lower 48 to make that wild place their home. I salute you.

## WHALEBONES AND CROSSES
(Joe Henry-Lee Holdridge)

Whalebones and crosses
Stand against the Arctic sky
The wind blows through the graveyard
Where our fallen fathers lie
Eternal snow that covers them
The shadows of the sun
The mighty struggle on the seas
A way of life is run

I'll sing for you my father
For the ancient sacred ways
How the hunter loved the hunted
How the night becomes the day
The circle of the mighty spirit
Keeps us in its fold
The warmth of understanding
Like a light shot through the cold

   Then bring to me my people
   Touch them with your loving hands
   Lead them from confusion
   Lead them back unto the land
   For a sickness seems to block their path
   It clouds my peoples' eyes
   The promise that an idle truth
   Will reap a golden lie

Whalebones and crosses
Stand against the Arctic sky
The wind blows through the graveyard
Where our fallen fathers lie
The timeless hunt a journey back
To what we once came from
Compassion and nobility
Beneath the midnight sun
   The mighty struggle on the seas
   A way of life is run

© 1977 Cherry Lane Music Co. (ASCAP)
Cherry River Music Co. (BMI)
Used by permission. All rights reserved.

## AMERICAN CHILD
(John Denver–Joe Henry)

   *Goin' up to Alaska*
   *Up to the land of the midnight sun*
   *Where the whale and the polar bear run*
   *O'er the icy blue sea*
   *Goin' up to Alaska*
   *Up to the north and the pioneer life*
   *Where courage and strength still survive*
   *And a man can be free*

American Child, does the call of the wild
Ever sing through the mist of your dreams
Does it fly with the wind when you waken again
When it's gone do you know what it means

Can you picture the time when a man had to find
His own way through an unbroken land
Before the machine changed the blue and the green
To something you can't understand

American Child, there's a burning inside you
That calls you away through the cold
To come back again to all that you've been
Can't you see that it's time to come home

To the flowers and trees and the rivers and the seas
And the earth who's the mother of all
A promise once made—will it shine, will it fade
Will we rise with the vision or fall

   *Goin up to Alaska*
   *Up to the land of the midnight sun*
   *Where the whale and the polar bear run*
   *O'er the icy blue sea*

   *Goin' up to Alaska*
   *Up to the north and the pioneer life*
   *Where courage and strength still survive*
   *And a man can be free*

   *Men can be free*
   *Goin' up to Alaska*
   *Goin' up to Alaska*
   *Goin' up to Alaska*

© 1977 Cherry Lane Music Co. (ASCAP)
Used by permission. All rights reserved.

## THE BALLAD OF ST. ANNE'S REEL
(David Mallett)

He was stranded in some tiny town
On fair Prince Edward Isle
Awaitin' for a ship to come and find him
A one-horse place, a friendly face
Some coffee and a tiny trace
Of fiddlin' in the distance far behind him

A dime across the counter then
A shy hello, a brand new friend
A walk along the street in the wintry weather
A yellow light, an open door
And a welcome friend, there's room for more
And then they're standing there inside together

> He said I've heard that tune before somewhere
> But I can't remember when
> Was it on some other friendly shore
> Or did I hear it on the wind
> Was it written on the sky above
> I think I heard it from someone I loved
> But I never heard it sound so sweet since then

Now his feet begin to tap
A little boy says I'll take your hat
He's caught up in the magic of her smile
And leap the heart inside him went
And off across the floor he sent
His clumsy body graceful as a child

> He said there's magic in the fiddler's arm
> There's magic in this town
> There's magic in the dancers' feet
> And the way they put them down
> People smilin' everywhere
> Boots and ribbons, locks of hair
> And laughter and old blue suits and Easter gowns

Now the sailor's gone, the room is bare
The old piano settin' there
Someone's hat's left hanging on the rack
And empty chairs, the wooden floor
That feels the touch of shoes no more
Awaitin' for the dancers to come back

And the fiddle's in the closet
Of some daughter of the town
The strings are broke and the bow is gone
And the cover's buttoned down
But sometimes on December nights
When the air is cold and the wind is right
There's a melody that passes through this town

© 1978 Cherry Lane Music Co. (ASCAP)
Used by permission. All rights reserved.

## YOU SAY THAT THE BATTLE IS OVER
(David Mallett)

> And you say that the battle is over
> And you say that the war is all done
> Go tell it to those
> With the wind in their nose
> Who run from the sound of the gun

And write it on the sides
Of the great whaling ships
Or on ice floes where conscience is tossed
With the wild in their eyes
It is they who must die
And it's we who must measure the loss

> And you say that the battle is over
> And finally the world is at peace
> You mean no one is dying
> And mothers don't weep
> Or it's not in the papers at least

There are those who would deal
In the darkness of life
There are those who would tear down the sun
And most men are ruthless
But some will still weep
When the gifts we were given are gone

Now the blame cannot fall
On the heads of a few
It's become such a part of the race
It's eternally tragic
That that which is magic
Be killed at the end of the glorious chase

From young seals to great whales
From waters to wood
They will fall just like weeds in the wind
With fur coats and perfumes
And trophies on walls
What a hell of a race to call men

> And you say that the battle is over
> And you say that the war is all done
> Go tell it to those
> With the wind in their nose
> Who run from the sound of the gun

And write it on the sides
Of the great whaling ships
Or on ice floes where conscience is tossed
With the wild in their eyes
It is they who must die
And it's we who must measure the loss
With the wild in their eyes
It is they who must die
And it's we who must measure the cost

© 1978 Cherry Lane Music Co. (ASCAP)
Used by permission. All rights reserved.

### IN MY HEART
(John Denver)

I don't know why
We still live together
We're so far apart
So much of the time
I don't know why
This beautiful weather
Is breaking my spirit
And tearing my mind all apart

Are you so lonely
Are you so sad
Have you lost your purpose
The faith that you had
If life is a question
I don't understand
If time is the reason
Then nobody can

   In my heart it is just an illusion
   It's not even real
   Much more than you think
   It's much more than you feel

My ears are still ringing
There's nothing to say
Why look to the ocean
To wash me away
There goes my best friend
There goes my last dime
If love is the answer
I'm wasting my time

   In my heart it is just an illusion
   It's not even real
   Much more than you think
   It's much more than you feel
   Do you feel
   Is this real
   How I feel
   In my heart

© 1979 Cherry Lane Music Co. (ASCAP)
Used by permission. All rights reserved.

### SONG FOR THE LIFE
(Rodney Crowell)

I don't drink as much as I used to
Lately it just ain't my style
And the hard times don't hurt like they ought to
They pass quicker like when I's a child

   Somehow I've learned how to listen
   For a sound like the sun goin' down
   In the magic the morning is bringing
   There's a song for the life I have found
   It keeps my feet on the ground

Don't the midsummer days sit so heavy
But don't they flow like a breeze through your mind
And nothin' occurs in a hurry
To make up for someone's lost time

   Somehow I've learned how to listen
   For a sound like the sun goin' down
   In the magic the morning is bringing
   There's a song for a friend I have found
   She keeps my feet on the ground

   Somehow I've learned how to listen
   For a sound like the breeze dyin' down
   In the magic the morning is bringing
   There's a song for the life I have found
   Keeps my feet on the ground

© 1976 Tessa Publishing Company (PRO)
Used by permission. All rights reserved.

**AUTOGRAPH**
(John Denver)

Here I am and closing my eyes again
Trying so hard not to see
All the things that I see
Almost willing to lie again
I swear that it just isn't so
It just isn't me

    We are never alone
    Even though we'd like to be

Then I go and open my eyes again
Love in your eyes is the thing
That I'd most like to see
I'd be willing to die again
To know of a place and a time
Where it always could be

    To be always with you
    And you always with me

This is my autograph
Here in the songs that I sing
Here in my cry and my laugh
Here in the love that I bring

    To be always with you
    And you always with me

Say a prayer and open your heart again
You are the love and the light
That we all need to see
Always willing to shine and then
Peace on this earth is the way
That it always can be

    To be always with you
    And you always with me

This is my autograph
Here in the songs that I sing
Here in my cry and my laugh
Here in the love that I bring

    To be always with you
    And you always with me

© 1979 Cherry Lane Music Co. (ASCAP)
Used by permission. All rights reserved.

# WHALEBONES AND CROSSES

Words by Joe Henry
Music by Lee Holdridge

C G A D A/C♯
5fr.
cov - ers them the sha - dows of the sun The might - y strug - gle
might - y spir - it keeps us in its fold The warmth of un - der -
Bm F♯m/A F♯7sus4 F♯7
1.
Bm
on the seas, A way of life is run.
stand - ing like A light shot through the
Em
I'll
2.
Bm
cold. Then
G A Bm C♯7sus4 C♯7
bring to me my peo - ple, touch them with your lov - ing hands

Lead them from con-fu-sion, _____ Lead them back un-to the land For a sick-ness seems to block their path it clouds my peo-ple's eyes The pro-mise that an i-dle truth _____ will reap a gold-en lie

*ad lib*   *a tempo*

Whale-bones and cross-es stand a-gainst the arc-tic sky The wind blows through the grave-yard where our fall-en fa-thers lie The time-less hunt a jour-ney back to what we once came from Com- pas- sion and no- bil- i- ty Be- neath the Mid- night Sun. The might- y strug- gle on the seas a way of life is run.

# IN MY HEART

Words and Music by
John Denver

Moderately slow

*mp flowing*

I don't know why_ we still live to-geth-er; We're so far a-part_ So much of the time._ I don't know why_ This beau-ti-ful weath-er Is break-ing my spir-it And tear-ing my mind_ all a-part.

© Copyright 1979 Cherry Lane Music Co.
This arrangement © Copyright 1980 Cherry Lane Music Co.
International Copyright Secured   All Rights Reserved

C
Fmaj7
Are you so lone - ly? Are you so sad? Have
ears are still ring - ing There's noth - ing to say. Why
you lost your pur - pose, The faith that you had? If
look to the o - cean To wash me a - way?
life is a ques - tion I don't un - der - stand, If
There goes my best friend, There goes my last dime; If
time is the rea - son, Then no - bod - y can.
love is the an - swer I'm wast - ing my time.
In my heart

*12 bar interlude omitted

# YOU SAY THAT THE BATTLE IS OVER

Words and Music by
David Mallett

Moderate Strum in one (𝅗𝅥. = 1 beat)

And you 1.4. say that the bat - tle is o -
2. say that the bat - tle is o -

- ver, and you say, that the war is all done.
- ver, and fin - 'lly the world is at peace.

Go tell it to those with the wind in their nose Who
You mean no one is dy - ing and moth - ers don't weep Or it's

© Copyright 1978 Cherry Lane Music Co.
This arrangement © Copyright 1980 Cherry Lane Music Co.
International Copyright Secured    All Rights Reserved

G/D G
C/G C
run from the sound of the gun. And write it on the
not in the pa - pers at least. There are those who would deal
C/G G
F/C C
sides of the great whal - ing ships. Or on ice floes where con - science is tossed.
in the dark - ness of life. There are those who would tear down the sun
C G
F C
With the wild in their eyes, it is they who must die And it's
And most men are ruth - less, but some will still weep When the
D
G
Last time to Coda
1.
G C/G G
C F/C C
we who must mea - sure the loss.
gifts we were giv - en are gone.
2. And you

2.
C/G F/C
D G
Em Am
D G
Em Am
G C
3. Now the blame can - not fall on the
C/G F/C
G C
D G
heads of a few, It's be - come such a part of the race.
It's e - ter - nal - ly trag - ic that that which is mag - ic Be

killed at the end___ of the glo - ri - ous chase.___ From young seals___ to great whales, from wa - ters to wood.___ They will fall just like weeds___ in the wind, With fur - coats___ and per - fumes___ and tro - phies on walls,___ What a hell of a race___ to call___ men.

*D.S. al Coda*

4. And you

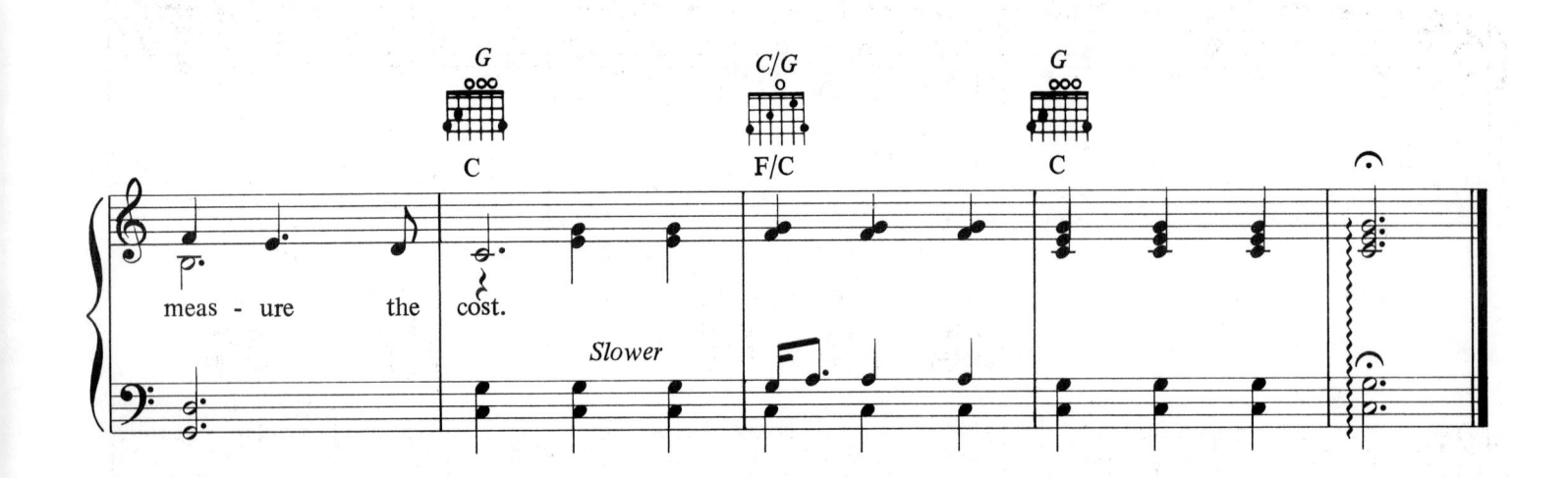

With the wild in their eyes ____ it is they who must die, ____ And it's we who must meas-ure the cost.

*Slower*

# AMERICAN CHILD

Words by Joe Henry
Music by John Denver

Moderately in 2 ($\dotted{\quarter} = 1$ beat)

Go-in' up to A-las - ka, up to the land of the Mid-night

© Copyright 1977 Cherry Lane Music Co.
This arrangement © Copyright 1980 Cherry Lane Music Co.
International Copyright Secured    All Rights Reserved

Sun, _____ Where the whale and the po-lar bear run o'er the i-cy blue sea. _____

Go-in' up to A-las-ka, up to the north and the pi-o-neer life, _____ Where cour-age and strength still sur-vive _____ and a man can be free.

A-mer-i-can Child, does the call of the wild ever sing thru the mist of your dreams? Does it fly with the wind when you wak-en a-gain? When it's gone do you know what it means? Can you pic - ture the time__ when a man had to find__ his own way through an un-brok-en land,__ Be - fore the ma-chine changed the blue and the green to some-thing you can't__ un - der - stand?__ A - mer - i - can Child, there's a burn - ing in - side you that calls you a - way__ through the cold To

come back a-gain___ to all that you've_ been, Can't you see___ that it's time to come

home _____ To the flow-ers and trees and the riv-ers and the seas and the

earth who's the moth-er of all? A prom-ise once made, will it

shine, will it fade, will we rise with the vi-sion or fall?_____ Go-in' up to A-

57

las - ka, up to the land of the Mid-night Sun, _____ Where the whale and the po-lar bear run o'er the i-cy blue sea. _____

Go-in' up to A-las - ka, up to the north and the pi-o-neer life, _____ Where courage and strength still sur-vive___ and a man can be free,___ Men can be free.___ Go-in' up to A-las-ka,___ Go-in' up to A-las-ka,___ Go-in' up to A-las-ka,___ Go-in' up to A-las-ka!___

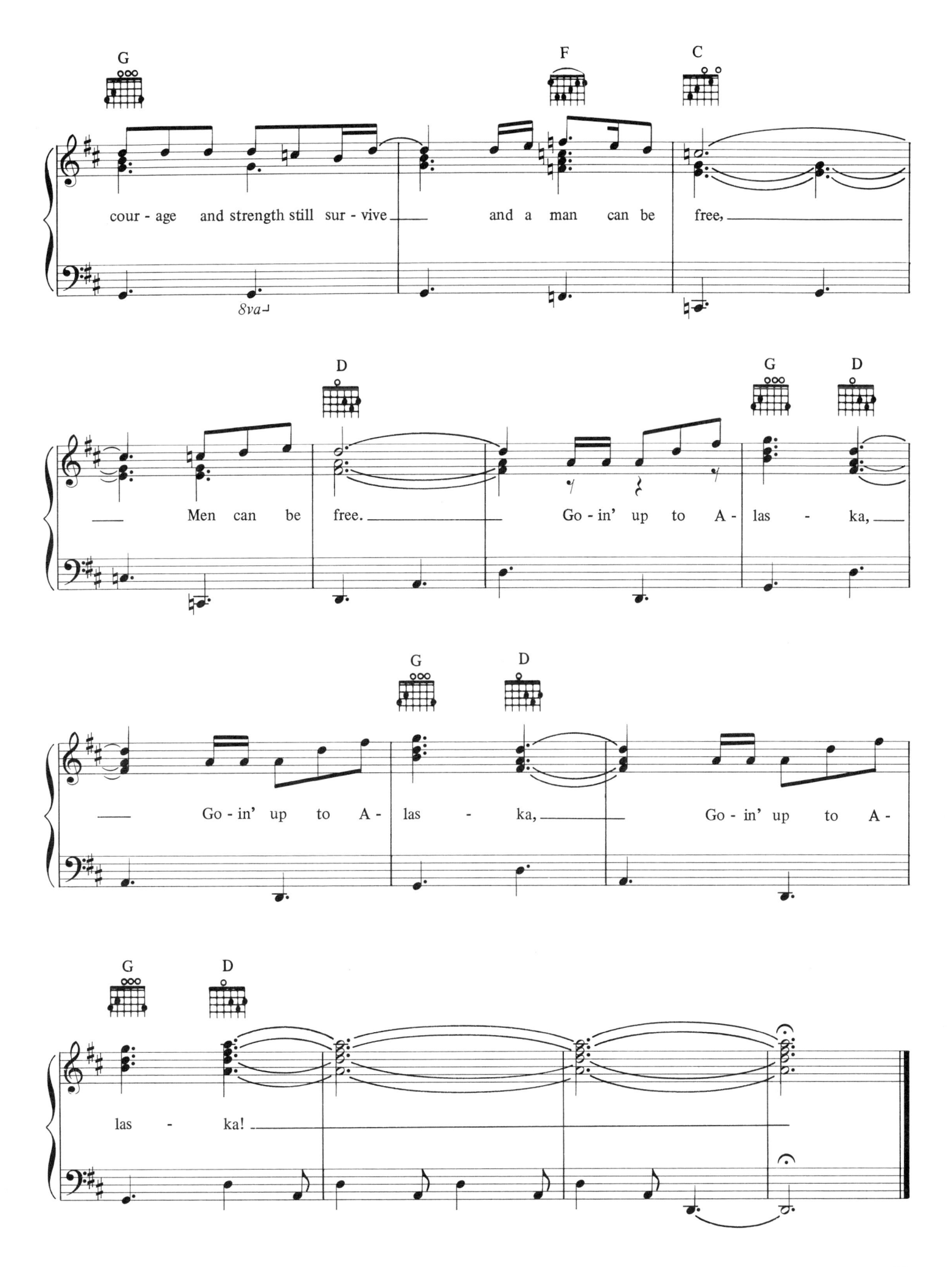

# AUTOGRAPH

Words and Music by
John Denver

Gentle rock beat, with feeling

Here I am, and clos-ing my eyes a - gain,
(Inst.)
Try-ing so hard not to see all the things that I see.
Al - most will-ing to lie a - gain, I

© Copyright 1979 Cherry Lane Music Co.
This arrangement © Copyright 1980 Cherry Lane Music Co.
International Copyright Secured   All Rights Reserved

swear that it just isn't so, It just isn't me. We are nev-er a-
lone e-ven tho' we'd like to be.
Then I go and o-pen my eyes a-gain,
Say a pray'r and o-pen your heart a-gain,
Love in your eyes is the thing that I'd most like to see.
You are the love and the light that we all need to see

61

G D/F♯ Em G7/D
3fr.
I'd be will-ing to die a-gain, To
Al-ways will-ing to shine and then
C G/B Am7 D
know of a place and a time where it al-ways could be;
Peace on this earth is the way that it al-ways can be
G D/F♯ Em G7/D
3fr.
3
To be al-ways with you, and
To be al-ways with you, and
C G/B Am7 G (short form) D
you al-ways with me.
you al-ways with me.

F♯o
G
3fr.
Am
D7
This is my aut - o-graph,
Here in the songs that I sing,
G
3fr.
F♯o
G
3fr.
Here in my cry and my laugh,
Am
D7
G
3fr.
D/F♯
Em
G7/D
3
Here in the love that I bring
To be al - ways with you, and
1.
C
G/B
Am7
G (short form)
D
you al - ways with me.
2.
C
G/B
Am7
G (short form)
D
you al - ways with me.
Slower

# JOHN DENVER ✤ Songbooks

*Edited by Milton Okun*

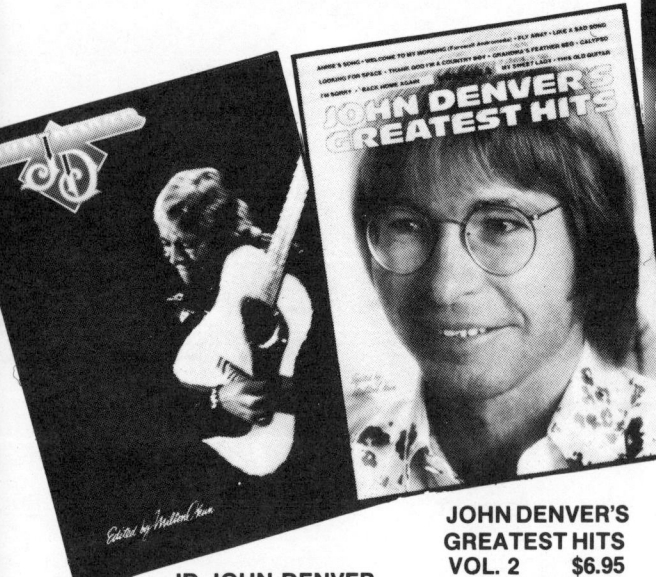

**JD JOHN DENVER**
$6.95

**JOHN DENVER'S GREATEST HITS VOL. 2**
$6.95

**AN EVENING WITH JOHN DENVER**
$7.95

**JOHN DENVER'S GREATEST HITS**
$6.95

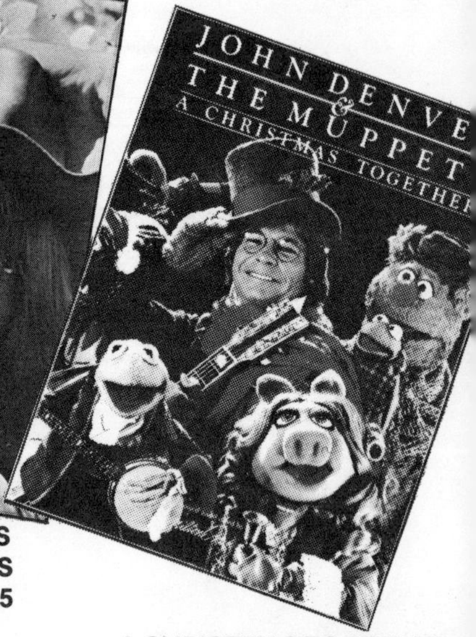

**A CHRISTMAS TOGETHER**
John Denver and The Muppets
$5.95

**FAREWELL ANDROMEDA**
$5.95

**THE JOHN DENVER SONGBOOK**
$6.95

**SPIRIT**
$5.95

**AERIE**
$3.95

**WINDSONG**
$5.95

**BACK HOME AGAIN**
$5.95

**ROCKY MOUNTAIN HIGH**
$5.95

**ROCKY MOUNTAIN CHRISTMAS**
$4.95

**I WANT TO LIVE**
$5.95

*Obtainable at your local music dealer or by sending check or money order to:*

**WINTER HILL MUSIC Ltd.** /P.O. Box 4247 • GREENWICH, CONNECTICUT 06830

(Please add 50¢ postage and handling plus sales tax where applicable). Free catalogue available upon request.